Babe! you look so fine I could drink y[...]
water!

Are you Jewish? Cause you ISRAELI HOT.

I love you like a pig loves not being bacon.

Hi, my name's James. Let's Bond.

Inheriting eighty million bucks doesn't mean much
when you have a weak heart.

Oh, so you breathe oxygen, too? We do have a lot
in common.

Your eyes are as blue as window cleaner.

Am I cute enough yet? Or do you need more to
drink?

The Ultimate Book of Cheesy Pick Up Lines

Well, here I am. What were your other two wishes?

Hi, will you help me find my lost puppy? I think he went into this cheap hotel room across the street.

What do you think of my shirt? It's made from boyfriend material.

You smell like trash. May I take you out?

Does this rag smell like chloroform to you?

Please tell your breasts to stop staring at my eyes

You are hotter than the bottom of my laptop!

Girl, you got more legs than a bucket of chicken.

I lost my teddy bear. Can I sleep with you tonight?

You're on Page 2 - have you found your favorite Pick Up Line Yet?

Tonight this Han doesn't want to fly Solo.

Shall we let only latex stand between our love.

You are like a candy bar: half sweet and half nuts."

You are so beautiful that I would marry your brother just to get into your family.

That's a nice dress. Can I talk you out of it?

I bet you $20 you're gonna turn me down.

My buddies bet me that I wouldn't be able to start a conversation with the most beautiful girl in the bar. Wanna buy some drinks with their money?

If I had to choose between one night with you or winning the lottery...I would chose winning the lottery...but it would be close...real close...

Hey, did you buy those pants on sale? Cuz at my place they're 100% off!

If you're going to regret this in the morning, we can sleep in until the afternoon.

If this bar was a meat market, you'd be the prime rib!

Get your coat; you've pulled.

What is a nice girl like you doing in a dirty mind like mine?

Can I read your T shirt in Braille?

Excuse me, I have a problem with my cell phone. Your number is not in it.

I'm learning about important dates in history class. Wanna be one of them?

The Ultimate Book of Cheesy Pick Up Lines

Excuse me, I think you have something in your eye. Oh wait, it's just a sparkle.

Your hand looks heavy. Let me hold it for you.

Kiss me if I'm wrong, but isn't your name Richard?

Are you into one-night stands? [No.] Then it's a good thing it's daytime.

Do you like short love affairs? I hate them. I've got all weekend!

If you were a chicken, you'd be impeccable.

Are you suffering from a lack of vitamin me?

Hey, are you the man that was going to buy me a beer?

The Ultimate Book of Cheesy Pick Up Lines

I need some answers for my math homework. Quick. What's your number?

Hi, I'm afraid of the dark. Would you mind sleeping with me?

I might as well call you "Google" 'cause you have everything I'm searching for.

A life without you, would be like a computer without an OS.

All those curves and me without brakes!

Are those diamonds real? [YES] I was talking about the ones in your eyes.

Are you from Paris? Because Eiffel for you!

Are you going to sleep with me or do I have to lie to my diary?

You're on Page 6 - have you found your favorite Pick Up Line Yet?

The Ultimate Book of Cheesy Pick Up Lines

Are you my Appendix? Because I have a funny feeling in my stomach that makes me feel like I should take you out.

Boy: Do you have any idea about the weight of a polar bear? Girl: How much? Boy: It's just enough to break the ice. I'm [name], by the way. May I know yours?

Do you believe in love at first sight or should I walk past you again?

Excuse me, are you from Tennessee? Girl: [No - Or why?] Boy: Because you're the only 10 that I see.

I can't think of anyone else I'd rather survive a Zombie Apocalypse with.

I don't know if you're beautiful, I haven't gotten past your eyes yet.

The Ultimate Book of Cheesy Pick Up Lines

I hear they banned you from school lunches for being so sweet.

I hope there's a fire truck nearby, cause you're smokin'!

I'd say God Bless you, but it looks like he already did.

I'm afraid of the dark… Will you sleep with me tonight?

I'm no mathematician, but I'm pretty good with numbers. Tell you what, Give me yours and watch what I can do with it.

I'm not staring at your boobs. I'm staring at your heart.

My doctor says I'm lacking Vitamin U.

People call me John, but you can call me tonight.

The Ultimate Book of Cheesy Pick Up Lines

Smile, if you want to sleep with me.

There are people who say Disneyland is the happiest place on earth. Apparently, none of them have ever been in your arms.

They say that kissing is a language of love. So, how about we have a conversation?

What's on the menu? Me-n-U

You know, I'm not really this tall. I'm just sitting on my wallet.

You like sleeping? Me too! We should do it together sometime!

You look cold. Do you want to use me as a blanket?

You must be the cure for Alzheimer's, because you're unforgettable.

You're on Page 9 - have you found your favorite Pick Up Line Yet?

The Ultimate Book of Cheesy Pick Up Lines

You see my friend over there? He wants to know if you think I'm cute

You: "How much does a polar bear weigh?" Her: "Uh, I don't know. How much?" You: "Enough to break the ice. Hi, I'm _____ "

You're definitely on my to-do list tonight.

Your smile is like Expelliarmus. Simple but disarming.

You're so hot, that if you ate a piece of bread, you'd poop out toast!

(You stepped on some ice.) Wow, now that the ice has finally broken, may I know your name?

"My love for you is like diarrhea, I just can't hold it in."

The Ultimate Book of Cheesy Pick Up Lines

"You're beautiful" has U in it, but "quickie" has U and I together.

(Ask a person for the time) 9:15? So today is May 1, 2008, at 9:15 PM, thanks I just wanted to be able to remember the exact moment that I met the woman of my dreams.

(hold out hand) Would you hold this for me while I go for a walk?

(in a Joey Tribiani accent) How you doin'?

(pick up a sugar packet off the floor) Uh, Miss? I see you dropped your name tag.

(Put your fingers on the other's nipples) Hey, here's (name), comin' at you with the weather. Can I be your warm front?

(Walk up to someone and bite them anywhere) Sorry, taking a bite out of crime. [WHAT?] Well it has to be illegal to look that good!

[As she's leaving] Hey, aren't you forgetting something? [What?] ME!!"

[Look at her shirt label.] When they say, "What are you doing?" You respond: "Yep! Made in heaven!"

[Point at her butt] Pardon me, is this seat taken?

"Hi, I'm writing a phone book, can I have your number?"

209. Do you work for a postal office? Because I could have sworn that you were just checking out my package.

A boy gives a girl 12 roses. 11 fake, 1 real and he says to her " I will stop loving you when all the roses die

A face without freckles is like a night sky without stars.

All because of you I cry much less, laugh a whole lot harder, and smile constantly.

Here's $10. Drink until I am really good looking, then come and talk to me.

Am I dead? Because I think I just met an angel.

Apart from being beautiful, what do you do in life?

Are those Guess jeans? 'Cause guess who wants to get into 'em.

Are those space pants? Because your butt is out of this world!

Are those things real?

Are you a 45 degree angle? Because you're acute-y!

Are you a 90 degree angle? 'Cause you are looking right!

Are you a banana? Because I find you a-peeling.

Are you a bank loan? Because you've got my interest

Are you a beaver? Cause daaaaam!

Are you a camera? Because every time I look at you, I smile.

Are you a campfire? Cause you are hot and I want s'more.

The Ultimate Book of Cheesy Pick Up Lines

Are you a carbon sample? 'Cause I want to date you.

Are you a cat? Cause you are purrrfect

Are you a dictionary? Cause you're adding meaning to my life.

Are you a florist? Cause ever since I met you, my life has been Rosey.

Are you a football player? Because I'd like you touchdown there!

Are you a fruit, because Honeydew you know how fine you look right now?

Are you a Gillette? Because you are the best a guy can get.

Are you a girl scout, cause you tie my heart in knots.

The Ultimate Book of Cheesy Pick Up Lines

Are you a hipster, because you make my hips stir.

Are you a horror movie? Because when I see you, my heart beats so fast.

Are you a jacket? Because I think I'm feeling cold, I would like to hug you.

Are you a keyboard? Because you're just my type.

Are you a kidnapper? Because you just abducted my heart.

Are you a light switch? 'Cause I want to turn you on!

Are you a magician? Because whenever I look at you, everyone else disappears!

Are you a magician??? Because Abraca-DAYUM!

You're on Page 16 - have you found your favorite Pick Up Line Yet?

The Ultimate Book of Cheesy Pick Up Lines

Are you a manhole? Because I easily fell for you.

Are you a microwave oven? Cause you melt my heart.

Are you a parking ticket? Because you've got FINE written all over you.

Are you a power button? You just turn me on.

Are you a Snickers bar? Cause you satisfy me.

Are you a supermarket sample? 'Cuz I wanna taste you again and again without any sense of shame.

Are you a tamale? 'Cause you're hot.

Are you a tangerine? 'Cause you certainly are a cutie.

The Ultimate Book of Cheesy Pick Up Lines

Are you a taxidermist? No? Do you want to try stuffing my pussy anyway?

Are you a terrorist? … cause you're the bomb!

Are you a vampire? Cause you looked a little thirsty when you looked at me.

Are you accepting applications for your fan club?

Are you African? Because you're a frican babe.

Are you an alien? Because you just abducted my heart.

Are you an interior decorator? Because when I saw you, the entire room became beautiful.

Are you an omelet? Because you're making me egg-cited!

The Ultimate Book of Cheesy Pick Up Lines

Are you an omelette? Because you're making me egg-cited!

Are you an orphanage? Cause I wanna give you kids.

Are you as beautiful on the inside as you are on the outside?

Are you Australian? Because you meet all of my koala-fications.

Are you being a ghost for Halloween, or are you just my boo?

Are you cake? Cause I want a piece of that.

Are you cold, do you need a jacket? Because you an jack it when we get back to my place.

Are you cold? You look like you could use some hot chocolate… Well, here I am!

The Ultimate Book of Cheesy Pick Up Lines

Are you drinking some hot tea? 'Cause you certainly are a hottie.

Are you feeling a little down? I can help feel you up.

Are you fertile? I need a favor. (Why?) I need a baby by next summer in order to get my inheritance

Are you free tonight, or will it cost me?

Are you from China? Because I'm China get your number.

Are you from Mexico? Because you're my Juan and only!

Are you from Russia? 'Cause you're Russian my heart rate!

Are you from Tennessee? Because you're the only ten I see!

Are you from Utah? 'Cause I want U-Tah date me.

Are you going to kiss me or do I have to lie about that part?

Are you Hurricane Katrina? Cause you're blowing me away.

Are you into one-night stands? [No.] Then why don't you lie down?

Are you Lana Del Rey? I just want to "la na del raise" your kids.

Are you lost ma'am? Because heaven is a long way from here.

Are you lost? Because heaven is a long way from here.

The Ultimate Book of Cheesy Pick Up Lines

Are you made of grapes? Cause you're fine as wine.

Are you married? If not, I'd like to marry you for one night.

Are you Mexican? Because you're my Juan and only!

Are you my phone charger? Because without you, I'd die.

Are you Netflix? Because I could watch you for hours.

Are you on Nickelodeon? Cause you're a-Dora-ble!

Are you ovulating? I need a favor cuz I need a baby within the year to get my inheritance.

Are you related to Dracula? Because you sure looked a little thirsty when you were looking at me.

Are you related to Jean-Claude Van Damme? Because Jean-Claude Van Damme you're sexy!

Are you religious? Because you're the answer to all my prayers.

Are you sitting on an F5 key? Because you're too refreshing.

Are you spaghetti cause I want you to meat my balls.

Are you sure you're not tired? You've been running through my mind all day.

Are you the delivery man? Because I believe you have a package for me.

The Ultimate Book of Cheesy Pick Up Lines

Are you the kind of guy who can look after himself or do you need a cute girl to take care of you?

Are you the moon? Because even when it's dark, you still seem to shine.

Are you the online order I placed a few days ago? 'Cuz I've been waiting for you all day.

Are you willing to take a pic with me? I want to get back at my ex.

Are you Willy Wonka's daughter, 'cuz you look sweet and delicious.

Are you working at Starbucks? That's because I like you a "latte."

Are your initials LSD? Cause you got me trippin

Are your legs made of Nutella? Because I'd love to spread them!

You're on Page 24 - have you found your favorite Pick Up Line Yet?

Are your parents bakers? Cause they sure made you a cutie pie!

Are your parents retarded, 'cause you sure are special.

Aside from being sexy what do you do for a living?

Babe, I need to tell you that you give brand new meaning to what "edible" means.

Babe, your beauty makes the morning sun look like the dull glimmer of the moon.

Baby I last longer than a white crayon.

Baby I might not be Sriracha sauce but, I sure will spice up your life.

Baby you make palms sweaty, knees weak, arms spaghetti.

The Ultimate Book of Cheesy Pick Up Lines

Baby, every time I see you, my cardiovascular system gets all worked up.

Baby, I like to wear you like a pair of sunglasses, one leg over each ear.

Baby, if you were words on a page, you'd be what they call *fine print*

Baby, I'm no Fred Flintstone, but I can make your Bedrock!

Baby, you are so fine I could put you on a plate and sop you up with a biscuit.

Baby, you must be tired because you've been running through my mind all night!

Baby, you're like a championship bass. I don't know whether to mount you or eat you.

The Ultimate Book of Cheesy Pick Up Lines

Baby, you're so hot, you make the equator look like the north pole.

Baby, you're so sweet, you put Hershey's outta business.

Bbrrrr! My hands are cold. Can I stick them down your pants to warm them up?

Be unique and different, say yes.

Because of you, I laugh a little harder, cry a little less, and smile a lot more.

Because you sure do give me a banana cream filling.

Before I try and hit on you please tell me if you have an issue with small genitalia.

Besides being gorgeous, what do you do for a living?"

You're on Page 27 - have you found your favorite Pick Up Line Yet?

The Ultimate Book of Cheesy Pick Up Lines

Blue eyes, red lips, pale face. So pretty. You look like the flag of France.

Boy: May I know your favorite color? Girl: [color?] Boy: Mine too! I guess we really are soul mates.

Brilliant Trick Melts Belly Fat Overnight (Do This Tonight)

Call me and I'll remind you how wonderful you are.

Call me Pooh, because all I want is you, honey.

Call me Shrek because I'm head ogre heels for you!

Can I be a secant line and lie tangent to your curves?

Can I borrow a kiss? I promise I'll give it back.

The Ultimate Book of Cheesy Pick Up Lines

Can I borrow a quarter? ["What for?"] I want to call my mom and tell her I just met the man/woman of my dreams.

Can I borrow your cell phone? I need to call animal control, because I just saw a fox!

Can I buy you a drink or do you just want the money?

Can I copy your dance moves?

Can I follow you home? Cause my parents always told me to follow my dreams.

Can I give you my number in case you are having a bad day?

Can I give you my number in case you're ever looking for a date who'll spoil you?

Can I have directions? [To where?] To your heart.

You're on Page 29 - have you found your favorite Pick Up Line Yet?

The Ultimate Book of Cheesy Pick Up Lines

Can I have your autograph?

Can I hit you in the face... with my lips?

Can I park my car in your garage? It's pretty big but it doesn't leak.

Can I put a smile in your inbox?

Can I take a picture of you to show Santa what I want for Christmas?

Can I take your picture to prove to all my friends that angels do exist?

Can I tell you your fortune? (take her hand and write your phone number on it.) Your future is clear.

Can I tie your shoes? I don't want you falling for anyone else.

You're on Page 30 - have you found your favorite Pick Up Line Yet?

The Ultimate Book of Cheesy Pick Up Lines

Can I walk through your bushes and climb your mountains?

Can we hold hands and practice falling in love?

Can we turn off the light so we could be the only one to be "on?"

Can you catch? because I think I'm falling in love with you.

Can you give me a tour of your body.

Can you please tell me how many seafood dinners it's going to take so I can transform your bedroom into an acrobat bedroom?

Can you please tell me what it feels like to look so amazing?

Can you pull this heart-shaped arrow out of my butt? A damn little kid with wings shot me.

The Ultimate Book of Cheesy Pick Up Lines

Can you take me home? I have nice bedside manners.

Can you take me to the bakery? Because, I want a Cutie pie like you!

Can you take me to the doctor? Because I just broke my leg falling for you.

Can you tell me how Heaven was when you last left?

Charizards are red, Squirtles are blue, if you were a Pokemon, I would choose you!

Come back to my place so I can give you a lovely parting gift.

Come live in my heart, and pay no rent.

Could I give you something to regret in the morning?

The Ultimate Book of Cheesy Pick Up Lines

Could you please step away from the bar? You're melting all the ice!

Damn girl, I thought diamonds were pretty until I laid my eyes on you!

Damn girl, you have more curves than a race track.

Damn lady, your ass is quite bigger than my future.

Damn! You with those curves and me without brakes!

Damn, are you my new boss, because you just gave me a raise.

Damn, I thought "Very-Fine" only came in a bottle!

Damn, if being sexy was a crime, you'd be guilty as charged!

You're on Page 33 - have you found your favorite Pick Up Line Yet?

Damn, I'm glad I'm not blind!

Dance? Well…Let me read you the story tonight when I tuck us into bed.

Darn girl you even look good with the lights on!

Did it hurt when you fell out of heaven?

Did it hurt? (Did what hurt?) When you fell out of heaven?

Did the sun come up or did you just smile at me?

Did we take a class together? No? I swore you and I had chemistry….

Did you bring your helmet? To prevent you getting a concussion when I bang you against the headboard tonight

The Ultimate Book of Cheesy Pick Up Lines

Did you clean your pants with Windex? I can practically see myself in them."

Did you die recently? Cause girl, you look like an angel to me.

Did you fart, cause you blew me away.

Did you get your license suspended for driving so many guys crazy?

Did you go to bed early last night? From the looks of it, you got your beauty sleep.

Did you have lucky charms for breakfast? Because you look magically delicious!

Did you invent the airplane? Cause you seem Wright for me.

Did you just come out of the oven? Because you're hot!

The Ultimate Book of Cheesy Pick Up Lines

Did you just see Star Wars? Because YODA one for me.

Did you just sit in a water puddle, or are you just happy to see me.

Did you just sit on a pile of sugar? Because you have a sweet ass.

Did you know I use pizza in the bedroom.

Did you know that before I left the rap game my stage name was Jenuine Rhyme…and I took Brooklyn by storm.

Did you know you make me melt like a popsicle in the hot summer sun?

Did you read Dr. Seuss as a kid? Because green eggs and... damn!

The Ultimate Book of Cheesy Pick Up Lines

Did you sit in a pile of sugar? Cause you have a pretty sweet ass.

Did your license get suspended for driving all these girls crazy?

Didn't I see you on the cover of Vogue?

Do I know you from somewhere? I think I do because you look just like my next lover.

Do I know you? (No.) That's a shame, I'd sure like to.

Do I know you? Cause you look exactly like my next girlfriend.

Do these look real? Wanna check?

Do you believe in love at first sight? Because I believe I've just fallen in love.

Do you believe in love at first swipe?

Do you believe in the hereafter? Well, then I guess you know what I'm here after.

Do you bleach your teeth? 'Cause your smile lights up the entire room like a candle in the dark. Let's go prove it.

Do you care for raisins? OK, what about a date then?

Do you drink Pepsi? Because you're so-da-licious!

Do you happen to have a Band-Aid? I scraped my knee falling for you.

Do you happen to have a map cuz babe I am getting lost in your eyes.

Do you have a bandage? I hurt my knee when I fell in love with you.

Do you have a Band-Aid? Because I just scraped my knee falling for you.

Do you have a jersey? 'Cause I need your name and number.

Do you have a map? Because I keep getting lost in your eyes.

Do you have a name or can I call you mine?

Do you have a name or can I just call you mine?

Do you have a pencil? Cause I want to erase your past and write our future.

Do you have a phone in your back pocket? Because your booty is calling me.

Do you have a sunburn, or are you always this hot?

The Ultimate Book of Cheesy Pick Up Lines

Do you have a twin sister? Then you must be the most beautiful girl in the world!

Do you have a void in your life I can fill?

Do you have advanced radiation poisoning? Because you are glowing!

Do you have an inhaler? Because you took my breath away!

Do you have any raisins? [No] How about a date?

Do you have any sunscreen? 'Cause you are burning me up!

Do you have rubbers at your house or should I pull out?

Do you have something stuck in your eye? Oh, never mind, it's just your sparkle.

Do you have the time? [Tells you the time] No, the time to write down my number?

Do you know how to use a whip?

Do you know karate? Because your body is really kickin'.

Do you know someone who repairs or sells a watch? I think my watch is damaged. If I'm with you, my time stops.

Do you know what I did last night? I looked up at the stars, and matched each one with a reason why I love you.

Do you know what I want to be for Halloween? I want to be your boyfriend/girlfriend.

Do you know what would look really good on you? Me.

The Ultimate Book of Cheesy Pick Up Lines

Do you know what? Blood is red. But I get tachycardia when I'm with you.

Do you like bacon? Wanna strip?

Do you like bananas or blueberries? Why? I wanna know what kind of pancakes to make in the morning.

Do you like jigsaw puzzles? Let's go to my room and put our pieces together.

Do you like Mexican food? Cause I want to wrap you in my arms and make you my BAE-RITTO.

Do you like Nintendo? Because Wii would look good together.

Do you like raisins? Well how about a date then?

Do you like sleeping? Me too. We should do it together sometime.

The Ultimate Book of Cheesy Pick Up Lines

Do you like Star Wars? Because Yoda only one for me!

Do you like to eat Mexican? Because you're heating up my taco.

Do you like whales? Well I have a hump-back at my place.

Do you like your eggs scrambled or fertilized?

Do you live in a corn field, cause I'm stalking you.

Do you mind if we share this cab to my house?

Do you need help with anatomy. I know all the body parts.

Do you own McDonald's? Because I'm actually loving it.

The Ultimate Book of Cheesy Pick Up Lines

Do you play soccer? Because you're a keeper!

Do you remember me? [No.] Oh that's right, we've only met in my dreams.

Do you sleep on your stomach? [No] Can I?

Do you smoke pot? Because weed be cute together.

Do you wanna go halfsies on a baby?

Do you want to be my dirty little secret?

Do you want to do something that rhymes with truck.

Do you want to give me an Australian kiss? It's like French kissing but you're going down under.

The Ultimate Book of Cheesy Pick Up Lines

Do you want to go to In-and-Out for burgers or just in-and-out of me?

Do you want to pretend my legs are made of butter and spread them?

Do you want to see a picture of a beautiful person? (hold up a mirror).

Do you want to take a shower with me to conserve water?

Do you wash your panties with Windex? Because I can really see myself in them.

Do you work at Dick's? Cause you're sporting the goods.

Do you work at Starbucks? Because I like you a latte.

Do your eyes hurt? Because you have been looking right all day.

Do your legs hurt from running through my dreams all night?

Does your face work at McDonald's? Because I'm lovin' it!

Does your father sell diamonds? Because you are FLAWLESS!

Does your heart have a hole? Because I think I'm trapped inside you and I just can't find my way out.

Does your left eye hurt? Because you've been looking right all day.

Does your mum work in a cake shop? 'Cuz she made you such a cutie pie.

Don't let me be the one that got away

Don't sweat the petty things… pet the sweaty things!

Don't let this go to your head, but do you want some?

Don't stick out your tongue unless you intend to use it.

Dr. Phil said that I'm afraid of commitment. Would you like to help me prove him wrong?

Each time I'm with you, I have anaerobic respiration. You just take my breath away.

Either my eyes need checking or you're the best looking guy I've ever seen.

Even if there wasn't gravity on earth, I'd still fall for you.

The Ultimate Book of Cheesy Pick Up Lines

Even though there aren't any stars out tonight, you're still shining like one.

Ever slept in a $5000 bed? Want to?

Excuse me, are you a magnet? Because I feel so attracted to you.

Excuse me, but do you give head to strangers? [No] Well then, allow me to introduce myself.

Excuse me, but I DO think it's time we met.

Excuse me, but I think I dropped something. MY JAW!

Excuse me, but I'm new in town, can I have directions to your place?

Excuse me, but you dropped something back there" (What?) "This conversation, lets pick it up later tonight.

The Ultimate Book of Cheesy Pick Up Lines

Excuse me, can I have your name so I can stalk you on Facebook?

Excuse me, can you give me directions? Because I just got lost in your eyes.

Excuse me, could you please dial down your hotness, it's causing global warming

Excuse me, I don't want you to think I'm ridiculous or anything, but you are the most beautiful woman I have ever seen. I just felt like I had to tell you.

Excuse me, I just notice that you're suffering from a lack of vitamin ME.

Excuse me, I just noticed you noticing me and I just wanted to give you notice that I noticed you too.

Excuse me, I just pooped in my pants. Can I get in yours?

The Ultimate Book of Cheesy Pick Up Lines

Excuse me, I was just wondering—could I be the one you've been dreaming of?

Excuse me, I was wondering if you could cure me of my ridiculous obsession with love.

Excuse me, I'm a little short on cash, would you mind if we shared a cab home together?

Excuse me, I've seem to have lost my virginity, can I have yours?

Excuse me, I'd like to have kids someday, and I wanted to know how your parents created such a beautiful creature.

Excuse me, if I go straight this way, will I be able to reach your heart?

Excuse me, I'm lost... Can you take me home with you?

The Ultimate Book of Cheesy Pick Up Lines

Excuse me, is your name Earl Grey? Because you look like a hot-tea!

Excuse me, would you be a gentleman and push in my stool?

Excuse me, would you like a raisin? No? How about a date then?

Excuse me… Do you have a pen? [She says yes.] Good, write down my number.

Fascinating. I've been looking at your eyes all night long, 'cause I've never seen such dark eyes with so much light in them.

Fffffiiiiiirrrreeee! No doubt…when you yell fire you grab attention good or bad.

For a moment I thought I had died and gone to heaven. Now I see that I am very much alive, and heaven has been brought to me.

You're on Page 51 - have you found your favorite Pick Up Line Yet?

The Ultimate Book of Cheesy Pick Up Lines

For some reason, I was feeling a little off today. But when you came along, you definitely turned me on.

Forget about Spiderman, Superman, and Batman. I'll be your man.

Forget that! Playing doctor is for kids! Let's play gynecologist.

Four plus four equals eight, but you plus me equals fate.

Funny Pick Up Lines: Are you French because Eiffel for you.

Funny Romantic Phrases

Girl, if I were a fly, I'd be all over you, because you're the shit!

Girl, you're like MasterCard - absolutely priceless.

Girls are sexy, guys are fine I'll be your six if you'll be my nine!

Give me your name, so I know what to scream tonight

Give me your number now.

Good thing I brought my library card... 'cause I can't stop checking you out.

Great legs, what time do they open?"

Guess what I'm wearing? The smile you gave me!

Have sex with me and I promise never to talk to you again!

Have you always been this cute, or did you have to work at it?

The Ultimate Book of Cheesy Pick Up Lines

Have you been to the doctor lately? Cause I think you're lacking some Vitamin Me.

Have you ever seen a girl swallow an entire banana? [wink, wink]

Have you got any room for an extra tongue in your mouth?

Hello are you married? [Yes] Well I didn't hear you say "happily".

Hello gorgeous, wanna fall in love?

Hello how are you? [Fine] Hey, I didn't ask you how you looked!

Hello pretty, want to hang out?

Hello, hottie—wanna kiss?

Hello, I just noticed that you were noticing me. So, here I am to give you a notice that I noticed you, too.

Hello, I'm a thief, and I'm here to steal your heart."

Hello, I'm sorry. Were you talking to me? If not, well then, please start.

Hello, I'm a thief, and I'm here to steal your heart.

Hello, I'm doing a survey of what people think are the cheesiest pickup lines. So, do you pick 'Do you come here often?', 'What's your sign?', or 'Hello, I'm doing a survey of what people think are the cheesiest pickup lines.'?

Hello, you're so fine you're making me stutter. Wha-wha-wha-wha'ts yo-yo-your na-na-name?

The Ultimate Book of Cheesy Pick Up Lines

Hello. Are you taking any applications for a boyfriend?

Hello. Cupid called. He says to tell you that he needs my heart back.

Hello. I just wanted to tell you that you take my breath away.

Here I am! What're your next two wishes?

Here's 10 cents - ring home and tell your mum that you won't be coming home tonight!

Here's the key to my house, my car... and my heart.

Hershey's makes millions of kisses a day.. .all I'm asking for is one from you.

Hey babe what's up? If you were a spider, you would be a mommy long legs.

The Ultimate Book of Cheesy Pick Up Lines

Hey babe, wanna see my baby elephant?

Hey baby you're so fine you make me stutter, wha-wha-what's your name?

Hey baby, are you like Sprite because you make me want to obey my thirst.

Hey baby, do you want to play a lion? You go kneel right there and I'll throw you my meat.

Hey baby, I must be a light switch, cuz every time I see you, you turn me on!

Hey baby, I think you just made my two by four into a four by eight.

Hey baby, I'd like to herd by cattle in your fertile valley.

Hey baby, I'm kind of cold, can I use your thighs as earmuffs?

The Ultimate Book of Cheesy Pick Up Lines

Hey baby, want to play fireman? We can stop, drop, and roll.

Hey Baby, you want to come to my house and work on your math skills? We can add the bed, subtract the cloths, divide the legs and multiply!

Hey baby, you've got something on your butt - my eyes!

Hey baby. You got a jersey? [A jersey?…Why?] Because I need your name and number.

Hey gorgeous, is your name Wifi? Because I'm feeling a connection!

Hey honey, wanna twerk for me?

Hey I'm looking for treasure, Can I look around your chest?

Hey sweet stuff. What are you up to? I just want to snap your chat.

Hey you….Hey…I'm trying to chap with you!

Hey, baby, you're so fine you make me stutter. Wha-wha-what's your name?"

Hey, can you help me get to a Doctor? My heart keeps skipping a beat when I'm with you.

Hey, congratulations! You've just been voted as the Most Beautiful Woman in This Room. The grand prize is a night with me.

Hey, could you touch my arm? I want to tell my friends I've been touched by an angel.

Hey, Cupid called... he says to tell you he needs my heart back.

Hey, don't frown. You never know who could be falling in love with your smile.

Hey, don't I know you? Yeah, you're the girl with the beautiful smile.

Hey, give me your car keys… coz' you're driving me crazy

Hey, how are you? [Fine] Wait, I didn't ask how you looked!"

Hey, how did you do that? (What?) Look so good?

Hey, I didn't know angels flew so low.

Hey, I think somebody farted. Would you like to get out of here?

Hey, I think you dropped something. Girl: What? Boy: My jaw.

Hey, is it just me, or are we destined to be married?

Hey, look––even the leaves are falling for you!

Hey, this Halloween, how 'bout you and I being boyfriend and girlfriend?

Hey, tie your shoes, I don't want you to fall for anyone else.

Hey, what's going on? So what's happening little trouble maker? Please tell me what I need to do to get on your drunk dial list.

Hey, what's up gorgeous girl? Seriously terrified of your response.

Hey, what's up? Guess what? It's your lucky day. Out of all the girls here, I picked you."

The Ultimate Book of Cheesy Pick Up Lines

Hey, you should stop eating magnets. You're making me attracted to you

Hey, you work out?

Hey. You're pretty. I'm cute. Together, we'd be pretty cute.

Hey... Didn't I see your name in the dictionary under "Shazaam!"?

Hey... somebody farted. Let's get out of here.

Hi I'm Mr Right, somebody said you were looking for me?

Hi the voices in my head told me to come talk to you.

Hi there. Cupid just called and told me to tell you to please give me my heart back.

The Ultimate Book of Cheesy Pick Up Lines

Hi, are you Jamaican? Coz jer-makin-me-crazy.

Hi, can you help me practice French kissing?

Hi, did your license get suspended for driving all these guys crazy?

Hi, do I look like someone you could learn to love?

Hi, do you mind? I'm conducting a study of what people think are the worst but funniest pickup lines. Do you think it's "what's your sign?" "would you like a drink" or "hi, do you mind?

Hi, do you want to have my children? (assuming the answer is 'no'), OK then, can we just practice.

Hi, I was just talking to my friend and he was wondering whether you think I'm cute.

Hi, I'm a thief, and I'm here to steal your heart.

The Ultimate Book of Cheesy Pick Up Lines

Hi, I'm doing a survey of what people think are the worst cheesy pick up lines. So, do you think it's: 'Do you come here often?', 'What's your sign?', or 'Hi, I'm doing a survey of what people think are the worst pick up lines'?"

Hi, I'm homosexual. Do you think you're capable of converting me?

Hi, I'm Mr. Right. Someone said you were looking for me?

Hi, I'm new to this country and you are the prettiest sight I've seen so far.

Hi, I'm writing a term paper on the finer things in life, and I was wondering if I could interview you?

Hi, I've lost my teddy, do you think you could cuddle with me instead?

Hi, I'm husband material—don't you think?

You're on Page 64 - have you found your favorite Pick Up Line Yet?

Hi, I'm new in town. Can you give me directions to your place?

Hi, I'm writing a term paper on the finer things in life, and I was wondering if I could interview you?

Hi, my name is "Milk." I'll do your body good.

Hi, my name is Doug. That's "god" spelled backwards with a little bit of U wrapped up in it

Hi, my name is Pogo, want to jump on my stick?

Hi, my name's Ying. Will you be my Yang?

Hi, sorry I don't have an opening line but since you have an opening and I have a line..

Hi. You'll do!

The Ultimate Book of Cheesy Pick Up Lines

Hi…Has anyone ever told you that your eyes are the clearest blue just like the ocean? Cuz I can see right into your heart and soul.

Him: If a fat man puts you in a bag at night, don't worry I told Santa I wanted you for Christmas.

Him: Something is wrong with my cell phone. You: Oh really? What happened? Him: It's just that… your number's not in it.

Hiya good looking, whatcha got cookin?

Holy cow, your eyes look just like falling stars.

Honestly, I have never met anyone so striking!

How come you're not on top of a Christmas tree? I thought that's where angels belonged.

How does it feel to be the most beautiful girl here?"

How is your fever? [What fever?] Oh… you just look hot to me.

How much does a polar bear weigh? [How much?] Enough to break the ice... Hi, I'm (insert name here).

How much does it cost to date you? Cause damn, you look expensive!

How much woman can you handle?

How much? To buy your heart, baby.

How was heaven when you left it?"

I am lost, would you like to join me to find my house?

I am not trying to impress you but I am a batman.

The Ultimate Book of Cheesy Pick Up Lines

I am writing a new algorithm, and I need some test data. What are your measurements?

I bet your dad is an environmentalist because you are so eco-friendly.

I blame you for global warming… your hotness is too much for the planet to handle!

I can see you've been a bad boy. Time for you to go to my room.

I can't breathe, your beauty takes my breath away.

I can't move, you are so beautiful that you blind me.

I can't believe I've been hear the entire evening with all these beautiful people and the moment I find 'The One', all I have time to say is "good bye".

I could lay next to you forever... or until we decide to go eat.

I could use some spare change and you're a dime.

I couldn't think of a pick-up line good enough for you, so I just wanted to say "Hi!"

I didn't believed in heaven, until I saw you.

I didn't see any stars in the sky tonight, the most heavenly body was standing right next to me.

I didn't know that angels could fly so low!

I didn't see any stars in the sky tonight, the most heavenly body was standing right next to me.

I don't drive a car but I'd like to walk you home.

The Ultimate Book of Cheesy Pick Up Lines

I don't have a library card, but do you mind if I check you out?

I don't know which is prettier today, the water, the sky or your eyes.

I don't know you, but I think I love you already.

I don't need a spoonful of sugar to swallow you

I don't need Twitter, I'm already following you.

I don't know what you think of me, but I hope it's X-rated.

I don't know you, but I think I love you already.

I don't need a spoonful of sugar to swallow you.

I don't speak in tongues, but I kiss that way.

I enjoy doing maintenance, you look like someone I would like to tinker" around with.

I feel like you are premium coffee: bold, tall and strong.

I had a wet dream about you last night. Would you like to make it a reality?

I have amnesia – do I come here often?

I have an "owie" on my lip. Will you kiss it and make it better?

I have had a really bad day and it always makes me feel better to see a pretty girl smile. So, would you smile for me?

I have never had a dream come true until the day that I met you.

You're on Page 71 - have you found your favorite Pick Up Line Yet?

The Ultimate Book of Cheesy Pick Up Lines

I have to show you the prettiest girl I've ever seen. (show your phone with a front camera on).

I hear you've been a bad boy. Now go to MY room!

I heard that you're good at math. Would you help me replace my X without asking Y?

I hope I'm your menstruation. In that way, I can visit you monthly.

I hope you know CPR, because you take my breath away!

I hope you like coffee…because I always have Folgers in my Cup.

I hope you like dragons, because I'll be dragon my balls across your face tonight.

The Ultimate Book of Cheesy Pick Up Lines

I hope you've got a pencil because I just want to erase your past and write our future together.

I hope your day has been as beautiful as you are.

I hurt my lip, will you kiss it to make it feel better?

I just got dumped, and I think that you could make me feel better.

I just had to come talk with you. Sweetness is my weakness.

I just learned that I only have 12 hours to live. Please don't let me die a virgin.

I just need to tell you that you're so beautiful that you give reason for the sun to shine bright each day.

I just wanted to show this rose how incredibly beautiful you are!

You're on Page 73 - have you found your favorite Pick Up Line Yet?

The Ultimate Book of Cheesy Pick Up Lines

I know how to read your palm and what it says is that in my heart you'll give me a call very soon.

I know I'm a perfect stranger. So let me introduce myself. I'm _____. See? Now I'm just perfect.

I know I'm not an organ donor, but I'm totally happy giving you my heart.

I know if I died now I'd be happy because I just got a little taste of Heaven.

I know I'm not a grocery item but I can tell when you're checking me out.

I know milk does a body good, but baby, how much have you been drinking?

I know somebody who likes you but if I wasn't so shy, I'd tell you who.

The Ultimate Book of Cheesy Pick Up Lines

I know someone that's totally into you and if I wasn't so shy I'd tell you who she was.

I know where they give out free drinks... it's a place called "My House"!

I know you're busy today, but can you add me to your to-do list?

I like Legos, you like Legos, why don't we build a relationship?

I like you more than football on a Sunday.

I like you more than I like gaming.

I like your dress. It looks like it's made from girlfriend material.

I like your skirt. Can I touch its material?

The Ultimate Book of Cheesy Pick Up Lines

I lost my best friend, can I be yours?

I lost my blanket. Will you be one for me tonight?

I lost my number, can I have yours?

I lost my virginity. Can I have yours?

I love baseball so take me home, baby!

I love my bed but I'd rather be in yours.

I love your shirt. Is it made from boyfriend material?

I may not be a genie, but I can make your dreams come true.

I may not be Wilma Flinstone, but I can sure as hell make your bed rock.

The Ultimate Book of Cheesy Pick Up Lines

I may not have gotten your virginity, but can I at least have the box it came in?

I must be a snowflake, because I've fallen for you.

I must be dancing with the devil, because you're hot as hell.

I must be in a museum, because you truly are a work of art.

I must confess, I wish I was one of your teardrops so I could be in your eyes, slip down your cheek, and lie still on your lips.

I need a dollar, but I only have 90 cents… do you want to be my dime?

I need a favor. Can you please give me the direct route to your heart because I guess I've gotten lost in your eyes.

The Ultimate Book of Cheesy Pick Up Lines

I need to ask you something. Perhaps are you a middle Eastern dictator cuz I think there is some sort of political uprising in my pants.

I need to tell you something. Your eyes are so much bluer than the Pacific ocean and I'm totally lost at sea.

I need to tell you that from the moment I saw you I looked for a signature, because any masterpiece always has one.

I never need to see the sun again because your eyes light up my world.

I opened my fortune cookie today and your name was on it!

I play the field, and it looks like I just hit a home run with you.

The Ultimate Book of Cheesy Pick Up Lines

I really don't have a library card but can I please check you out?

I really hope there is a fireman around, because you are totally smoking hot!

I saw you and I kept humming, "You take my breath away, aye, aye. You take my breath away!"

I seem to have lost my phone number. Can I have yours?

I seriously want you to take me to brunch. Please don't bust my heart because brunch time is just about finished.

I sneezed because God blessed me with you.

I suffer from amnesia. Have we had sex before?

The Ultimate Book of Cheesy Pick Up Lines

I swear you must be a musician because every single time I look at you I know everything else just disappears.

I taste so delicious, you'll want the recipe!

I thank God that I'm wearing gloves now. Because you're just too hot to handle.

I think I can die happy now, cause I've just seen a piece of heaven.

I think I could fall madly in bed with you...

I think I love you but I can't be sure until I kiss you.

I think I should tell you what people are saying behind your back: "Nice butt!"

I think I've seen you before. Do you model?

I think my heart just lagged.

I think my lipstick tastes like chocolate, would you like to try it?

I think there's something wrong with my eyes because I can't take them off you.

I think there's something wrong with my phone. Could you try calling it for me to see if it rings?

I think you just stole something. [What's That?] My heart.

I think you owe me one drink. Because when I stared at you, I dropped mine.

I think you're Broca's Aphasia? Girl: Why? Boy: It's because you leave me speechless.

I think you're good at puzzle. Because my day just started but you've completed it already.

I thought happiness started with an H. Why does mine start with U?

I tried my best to not feel anything for you. Guess what? I failed.

I value my breath, so it'd be nice if you stopped taking it away every time you walked by.

I wanna live in your socks so I can be with you every step of the way.

I wanna take out your pencil and stick it in my pencil case.

The Ultimate Book of Cheesy Pick Up Lines

I want to ask if you'll date me without looking desperate. But PLEASE will you go out with me?

I want to be your high-heels so I can walk with you every ste of the way.

I want to be your tear drop, so I could be born in your eyes, live on your cheeks, and die on your lips.

I want to commit a crime where I will steal your heart, and you will steal mine.

I want to melt in your mouth, not in your hand.

I want to write a poem on your body with my lips.

I want you to treat me like a pirate and just give me your booty.

I wanted you to know… if you were a potato, you'd be a sweet one.

You're on Page 83 - have you found your favorite Pick Up Line Yet?

I was all set to say something really sweet about you but when I caught a glimpse of you I was totally speechless.

I was blinded by your beauty... I'm going to need your name and number for insurance purposes.

I was feeling a little off today, but you definitely turned me on.

I was so content with my life and one day I asked God, what could be better than this? And then I met you.

I was so enchanted by you that I ran into that wall over there. So I am going to need your name and number for insurance purposes.

I was thinking of calling heaven and asking for an angel but what I really want is a bad girl.

The Ultimate Book of Cheesy Pick Up Lines

I was wondering if you had an extra heart? Mine seems to have been stolen

I was wondering if you have a moment to spare for me to hit on you?

I will stop loving you when an apple grows from a mango tree on the 30th of February.

I wish I was cross eyed, so I could see you twice.

I wish I was your derivative so I can lie tangent to your curve.

I wish I were an octopus. In that way, I would have eight hands to touch you.

I won't give you a cheesy pick up line, if you let me buy you a drink.

I would die a million deaths if it meant I could be with you.

You're on Page 85 - have you found your favorite Pick Up Line Yet?

I would flirt with you, but I'd rather seduce you with my awkwardness.

I would marry your cat if that's what it takes to be part of your family.

I would offer you a cigarette, but you're already smokin' hot.

I'd like to be your boss. Because it's okay for me to be a slave of your love.

I'll be Burger King and you be McDonald's. I'll have it my way, and you'll be lovin' it.

I'll cook you dinner if you cook me breakfast.

I'll give you a nickel if you tickle my pickle.

I'll make you shiver when I deliver.

The Ultimate Book of Cheesy Pick Up Lines

I'll marry you tomorrow, but let's honeymoon tonight.

I'll show you my tan lines if you show me yours.

I'm a freelance gynecologist. How long has it been since your last checkup?

I'm a member of a boy band known as "Wrong Direction."

I'm a zombie, can I eat you?

I'm against animal cruelty. Please don't hurt my monkey, stroke it gently.

I'm an astronaut and my next mission is to explore Uranus.

I'm certain your heart stops when you sneeze. The same thin that happens when I'm pondering you.

I'm drowning in the sun and need mouth to mouth now!

I'm easy. Are you?

I'm fighting the urge to make you the happiest woman on earth tonight."

I'm going to give you a kiss. If you don't like it, just return it.

I'm going to have to ask you to leave. You're making everyone else look bad.

I'm going to kiss you now. Say 'Kiss Me' if you want me to stop

I'm in a Boyband called Wrong Direction

I'm in the mood for pizza... a pizza you, that is!

The Ultimate Book of Cheesy Pick Up Lines

I'm invisible. (Really?) Can you see me? (Yes) How about tomorrow night?

I'm just wondering here. Would your lips taste as good as they look? I would like to try them.

I'm like a delicious pizza. The best part is the sausage on top.

I'm lonely, can you keep me company tonight at my place?

I'm Mr. Right, someone said you were looking for me?

I'm new in town, could I have the directions to your house please?

I'm new in town. Could you give me directions to your apartment?

I'm no Fred Flintstone but I can make your bed rock.

I'm no organ donor but I'd be happy to give you my heart.

I'm no photographer, but I can picture us together.

I'm no weather man, but you can expect a few inches tonight.

I'm not a hoarder but I really want to keep you forever.

I'm not a photographer, but I can picture you and me together.

I'm not actually this tall. I'm sitting on my wallet.

I'm not drunk, I'm just intoxicated by you."

The Ultimate Book of Cheesy Pick Up Lines

I'm not staring, I'm just stuck in a loop.

I'm not too good at algebra, but doesn't U+I = 69?

I'm not trying to impress you or anything, but…
I'm Batman!

I'm on fire. Can I run through your sprinkler?

I'm on top of things. Would you like to be one of them?

I'm pretty great at Algebra; I can make your X disappear and you'll never need to know Y.

I'm sorry were you talking to me? "No" then please start!

I'm sorry, I don't think we've met. I wouldn't forget a pretty face like that.

I'm sorry, were you talking to me?" [No.] "Well then, please start.

I'm the kind of man who deserves to have women I don't deserve.

I'm thinking you must have just come out of the oven because you are incredibly hot!

I'm thinking you're a robber because you just totally stole my heart.

I'm wearing Revlon Colorstay Lipstick, want to help me test the claim that it won't kiss off?

I've been abstaining for the past few years and just looking to get back out there and get my feet wet.

I've got a question for you. Don't you think we would look fantastic on a wedding cake together?

I've got an alarm clock that makes the best sound in the morning. Would you like to come and hear it?

I've heard you like water. That's good – you already like 70% of me.

I've lost that loving feeling, will you help me find it again?

I'd say God Bless you, but it looks like he already did.

If a fat man puts you in a bag at night, don't worry I told Santa I wanted you for Christmas.

If a thousand painters worked for a thousand years, they could not create a work of art as beautiful as you.

If beauty were time, you'd be eternity.

The Ultimate Book of Cheesy Pick Up Lines

If God made anything more beautiful than you, I'm sure he'd keep it for himself.

If I could reach out and hold a star for everytime you've made me smile, I'd hold the sky in the palm of my hand.

If I could rearrange the alphabet, I'd put U and I together.

If I flip this coin, what are my chances of getting either head or tail?

If I followed you home, would you keep me?

If I had a nickel for every time I saw someone as beautiful as you, I'd have 5 cents

If I had a penny for every time I thought of you, I'd have exactly one cent, because you never leave my mind.

The Ultimate Book of Cheesy Pick Up Lines

If I had a rose for each thought I had of you I would never ever want to leave my garden.

If I had a rose for every time I thought of you, I would be walking through my garden forever.

If I had a star for every time you brightened my day, I'd have a galaxy in my hand."

If I had to choose between breathing or loving you, I would say "I love you" with my last breath!

If I promise to catch you, would you fall for me?

If I received a nickel for every time I saw someone as beautiful as you, I'd have exactly five cents.

If I told you I work for UPS, would you let me handle your package?

If I told you, you had a gorgeous body, would you hold it against me?

The Ultimate Book of Cheesy Pick Up Lines

If I was a super hero, I'd be BlanketMan, 'cause I got you covered.

If I was a watermelon, would you spit my seed?

If I was an octopus, all my 3 hearts would beat for you☐.

If I was an operating system, your process would have top priority.

If I was in charge of rewriting the alphabet, I'd make sure U and I were right beside each other.

If I were a cat I'd spend all 9 lives with you.

If I were a dog would you help me bury my bone.

If I were a stop light, I'd turn red everytime you passed by, just so I could stare at you a bit longer.

The Ultimate Book of Cheesy Pick Up Lines

If I were a transplant surgeon, I'd give you my heart.

If I were the king, and you were the queen, in the cosmic game of chess, would you mate with me?

If I were to ask you for sex, would your answer be the same as the answer to this question?

If I were to ask you out on a date, would your answer be the same as the answer to this question?"

If I'm vinegar, then you must be baking soda. Because you make me feel all bubbly inside!

If Internet Explorer is brave enough to ask you to be your default browser, I'm brave enough to ask you out!

If it weren't for that DAMNED sun, you'd be the hottest thing ever created.

You're on Page 97 - have you found your favorite Pick Up Line Yet?

The Ultimate Book of Cheesy Pick Up Lines

If kisses were snowflakes, I'd send you a blizzard

If looks could kill you would be a weapon of mass destruction

If nothing lasts forever, will you be my nothing?

If stars would fall every time I would think of you, the sky would soon be empty.

If the sun were to stop shining, I'd be your source of vitamin D.

If there were only one chocolate left in this world, I would give it to you just to see your enjoyment.

If we shared a garden, I'd put my tulips and your tulips together. (tulips = two lips)

If women were trophies, you'd be first place!

You're on Page 98 - have you found your favorite Pick Up Line Yet?

The Ultimate Book of Cheesy Pick Up Lines

If you are love-starved can I be your smorgasbord?

If you could put a price tag on beauty you'd be worth more than Fort Knox.

If you stood in front of a mirror and help up 11 roses, you would see 12 of the most beautiful things in the world.

If you want me, don't shake me, or wake me, just take me.

If you were a booger I'd pick you first.

If you were a burger at McDonald's you'd be the McGorgeous

If you were a burger, you'd be McDelicious!

If you were a drug, I would overdose!

The Ultimate Book of Cheesy Pick Up Lines

If you were a Facebook status, I would like you.

If you were a flower you'd be a damnnn-delion

If you were a fruit, you'd surely be a "fineapple."

If you were a hamburger at McDonald's, you'd be a McGorgeous.

If you were a laser you would be set on stunning.

If you were a McDonald's burger, you'd be McBeautiful.

If you were a new sandwich at McDonalds, you'd be called McHandsome.

If you were a potato you'd be a sweet one.

If you were a steak you would be well done.

The Ultimate Book of Cheesy Pick Up Lines

If you were a tear drop, I would never cry for fear of losing you.

If you were a tear in my eye I would not cry for fear of losing you.

If you were a transformer, you'd be a HOT-obot, and your name would be Optimus Fine.

If you were a triangle, you'd be acute one.

If you were a tropical fruit, you'd be a Fine-apple!

If you were a vegetable you'd be a cute-cumber.

If you were ground coffee, you'd be Espresso cause you're so fine.

If you were in bed with me, I wouldn't need the cover to keep warm.

The Ultimate Book of Cheesy Pick Up Lines

If you were to be a potato, you would be a sweet one.

If you were words on a page, you'd be what they call "fine print."

If you worked at "build-a-bear" I'd stuff you right now.

If you're advertising, I'm buying!

If you're feeling down, I can feel you up.

If your heart was a prison, I would like to be sentenced for life.

If you're having a love drought, can I be your rain?

If you're traveling this journey of life alone, can I be your +1?

The Ultimate Book of Cheesy Pick Up Lines

If you've been looking for love, consider yourself found!

I'll cook you dinner if you cook me breakfast.

I'm fighting the urge to make you the happiest woman on earth tonight.

I'm going to have to call the cops, because you just stole my heart!

I'm going to regret every day of my life if you're not in it.

I'm looking for a new girlfriend, would you be interested?

I'm lost. Can you tell me which road leads to your heart?

I'm new in town. Could you give me directions to your apartment?

The Ultimate Book of Cheesy Pick Up Lines

I'm no organ donor but I'd be happy to give you my heart.

I'm no photographer but I sure could picture us together.

I'm no sailor but I'm sure I could float your boat!

I'm not a horse, but you can ride me like one if you like.

I'm not a photographer, but I can picture me and you together.

I'm not actually this tall. I'm sitting on my wallet.

I'm not drunk, I'm just intoxicated by you.

I'm not trying to impress you or anything, but... I'm Batman!

The Ultimate Book of Cheesy Pick Up Lines

I'm sorry, I don't think we've met. I wouldn't forget a pretty face like that.

I'm sorry, were you talking to me? [No] Well then, please start.

In my mind, we're going to have sex anyway, so you might as well be in the room.

Is it hot in here or is it just you?

Is it okay to take a photo of you? I just want to show my friends that angels are indeed real.

Is that a ladder in your stockings or the stairway to heaven?

Is that a mirror in your pocket? Cause I can see myself in your pants!

Is there a rainbow today? Because I just found the treasure I've been searching for!

The Ultimate Book of Cheesy Pick Up Lines

Is there a science room nearby or am I sensing some chemistry?

Is there an airport nearby or is that just my heart taking off?"

Is your body from McDonald's? Cause I'm lovin' it!

Is your car battery dead? Because I'd like to jump you.

Is your dad a drug dealer? Cause you're so Dope!

Is Your Dad A Preacher? Cause Girl You're A Blessing.

Is your dad a terrorist? Because you are the bomb!

Is your dad an art thief? Because you're a rare masterpiece.

You're on Page 106 - have you found your favorite Pick Up Line Yet?

The Ultimate Book of Cheesy Pick Up Lines

Is your dad the muffin man?

Is your daddy a Baker? Because you've got some nice buns!

Is your father a fireman? Because you are just so hot!

Is your father a mechanic? Because you've got a finely tuned body!

Is your father a thief? Because someone stole the stars from the sky and put them in your eyes.

Is your father Little Caesar? Cause you look Hot 'n Ready.

Is your last name Campbell? Cause you're "mmmm... good!"

Is your last name Gillette? Because you are the best a man can get.

You're on Page 107 - have you found your favorite Pick Up Line Yet?

The Ultimate Book of Cheesy Pick Up Lines

Is your last name is Jacobs? Because you're a real cracker.

Is your last name Whitman, because I want to sample you.

Is your name "swiffer"? 'Cause you just swept me off my feet.

Is your name Ariel? Cause we Mermaid for each other!

Is your name daisy? Because I have a sudden urge to plant you right here.

Is your name Dora? Cause I'll let you explore..

Is your name Dunkin? Because I Donut want to spend another day without you.

Is your name Dwayne Johnson? Because you Rock my world!

Is your name Google? Because you have everything I've been searching for.

Is your name Katrina? [No, why?] 'Cuz baby, you rock me like a hurricane!

Is your name Mickey? Because you're so FINE!

Is your name Summer? Because you are so hot.

Is your name Wi-Fi? Because I'm really feeling a connection.

Is your nickname Chapstick? Because you're da balm!

It looks like you dropped something - my jaw!

It's a ncw world order. Have your way with me.

The Ultimate Book of Cheesy Pick Up Lines

It's not my fault I fell in love. You are the one that tripped me.

It's not the size of the boat. It's the motion of the ocean.

It's probably your fault that there is global warming.

It's a good thing I wore gloves today. Otherwise you'd be too hot to handle.

It's dark in here. Wait! It's because all of the light is shining on you.

I've been a bad girl, so spank me!

I've been waiting all my life to meet someone like you, so I had to come and say hello.

I've got the buns. Have you got the hot dog?

The Ultimate Book of Cheesy Pick Up Lines

I've heard sex is a killer. Want to die happy?

Just where do those legs of yours end?

Kiss me if I'm wrong, but dinosaurs still exist, right?

Kissing burns 5 calories a minute. How about a workout?

Know what's on the menu? Me 'n' u.

Let me insert my plug into your socket and we can generate some electricity.

Let me tie your shoes, cause I don't want you falling for anyone else.

Let's be nothing. 'Cause nothing lasts forever.

The Ultimate Book of Cheesy Pick Up Lines

Let's commit the perfect crime: I'll steal your heart, and you steal mine.

Let's go to my place and do the things I'll tell everyone we did anyway.

Let's have breakfast together tomorrow; shall I call you or nudge you?

Let's make like fabric softener and snuggle.

Let's make out so I can see if you taste as good as you look!

Let's play circus. First sit on my face, I will guess your weight and then I will eat the difference.

Let's play hockey. I'll be the net, and you can score.

Let's play house. You can be the door and I can slam you all I want!

The Ultimate Book of Cheesy Pick Up Lines

Let's play Winnie the Pooh and get my nose stuck in your honey jar.

Let's save water by taking a shower together.

Let's commit the perfect crime: I'll steal your heart, and you'll steal mine.

Let's do breakfast tomorrow. Should I call you or nudge you?

Let's make like the Olympic rings and hook up later.

Let's play hockey. I'll be the net, and you can score.

Let's play Winnie the Pooh and get my nose stuck in your honey jar.

Let's see how long it takes you.

The Ultimate Book of Cheesy Pick Up Lines

Lie down on your couch and pretend that your legs hate each other.

Life without you would be like a broken pencil… pointless.

Like Motel 6, I'll leave the light on for you.

Love your picture. Big thanks. Do you want to eat cookie dough sometime together?

May I ask you something? Besides being beautiful, what else do you do for a living?

May I end this sentence with a proposition?

May I flirt with you?

May I know how it feels to be the most gorgeous woman here?

The Ultimate Book of Cheesy Pick Up Lines

Me love you long time.

Me without you is like a nerd without braces, A shoe without laces, aSentenceWithoutSpaces

Most guys need 3 meals a day to keep going… I just need eye contact from you.

Most people like to watch the Olympics, because they only happen once every 4 years, but I'd rather talk to you cause the chance of meeting someone so special only happens once in a lifetime.

My attraction to you is an inversed square law.

My bed is broken, can I sleep in yours?

My bedroom has a very interesting ceiling.

My dad told me life is just like a deck of cards, which means you've got to be the queen of hearts.

The Ultimate Book of Cheesy Pick Up Lines

My ex-girlfriend used to call me Goldfinger.

My family has a history of high blood sugar, but I still want you even though you're really sweet

My friend thinks you're kinda cute, but I don't... I think you're absolutely gorgeous!

My lenses turn dark in the sunshine of your love.

My lips are like skittles. Wanna taste the rainbow?

My love for you is like diarrhea, I just can't hold it in.

My magic watch says that you aren't wearing any underwear. (She says she does) Damn! it must be 15 minutes fast

My mom and dad brought me up to be a good girl but tonight I feel like breaking the rules and getting a little naughty.

You're on Page 116 - have you found your favorite Pick Up Line Yet?

The Ultimate Book of Cheesy Pick Up Lines

My name is (your name) but you can call me tonight.

My name is _____. Remember that, you'll be screaming it later.

My name isn't Elmo, but you can tickle me any time you want to.

My name may not be Luna, but I sure know how to Lovegood!

Next time you think of beautiful things don't forget to count yourself in.

Nice beach balls, can I play?

Nice hair, wanna mess it up?

Nice legs, what time do they open?

The Ultimate Book of Cheesy Pick Up Lines

Nice package. Let me unwrap that for you.

Nice pants. Can I test the zipper?

Nice shirt! What's it made out of, boyfriend material?

Nice to meet you, I'm (your name) and you are...gorgeous!

No ring? You should be someone's husband

No wonder the sky is grey today, all the blue is in your eyes.

Not sure what your name is but I'm sure it is as beautiful as you are!

Now I know why they call it a beaver, because I'm dying for your wood.

The Ultimate Book of Cheesy Pick Up Lines

Of all the beautiful curves on your body, your smile is my favorite.

Oh no, I'm choking! I need mouth to mouth, quick!

Oh, you're a fan of Spider man, superman and batman? How about I'll be your man?

Oh, you're from Tennessee? [No.] Well, you're definitely the only TEN-I-SEE.

Okay I'm here. What were your other two wishes?

On a scale from one to ten, how old are you?

On a scale of 1 to 10, you're a 9. I'm the 1 you need.

On a scale of 1 to America, how free are you tonight?

The Ultimate Book of Cheesy Pick Up Lines

One-Living in the now is magical. Let's just go out on a date.

Ouch! My tooth hurts! [Why?] Because you are soooo sweet!

Our break-up is worse than traffic in NY. I can't move-on!

Pick a number between 1 and 10. Sorry you lost, you'll have to take off all your clothes.

What kind of Uber are you – long or short rides?

Pinch me. [Why?] You're so fine I must be dreaming.

Please call 9-1-1, because you just made my heart stop!

Please call an ambulance, your beauty is killing me.

The Ultimate Book of Cheesy Pick Up Lines

Please drink up until I'm really good looking—
then come chat with me.

Please excuse me…I'm creating an easy on the
finest things in life, and I was wondering if you
had a few minutes for me to interview you.

Please keep your distance. I might fall for you.

Please tell me, on a scale of one to America, how
available are you this evening?

Please tell me…If I was your heart would you let
me beat.

Put down that cupcake... you're sweet enough
already.

Rejection can lead to emotional stress for both
parties involved and emotional stress can lead to
physical complications such as headaches, ulcers,

You're on Page 121 - have you found your
favorite Pick Up Line Yet?

cancerous tumors, and even death! So for my health and yours, JUST SAY YES!

Remember Him? He Was A Huge Star Before His Plastic Surgery

Roses are red and brown is the tree—I was wondering if you'd go out with me.

Roses are red and so are your lips—let's get on the dance floor and wiggle our hips!

Roses are red and violets are blue, I'd really love to go out with you.

Roses are red, I have a crush, whenever I'm around you, all I do is blush.

Roses are red, my face is too, that only happens when I'm around you.

You're on Page 122 - have you found your favorite Pick Up Line Yet?

Roses are red, violets are fine. If I be the 6, will you be the 9?

Santa's lap is not the only one wishes come true.

Save water, shower with a friend.

See my friend over there? He wants to know if you think I'm cute.

See that door? Let's go out.

See these keys? I wish I had the one to your heart.

Sex is a killer. Do you wanna die happy?

Sex is evil, evil is sin, sins are forgiven, so stick it in.

She/He says: "Hold on"

The Ultimate Book of Cheesy Pick Up Lines

Should I smile because we are friends, or cry because I know that is what we will ever be?

Smile. It is the second best thing you can do with your lips.

Smoking is hazardous to your health… and baby, you're killing me!

So apparently we both have fantastic taste. So this is to you and me. I'm doing all the talking and you are just sitting looking pretty.

So happy I'm wearing gloves because you're way too hot to handle.

So last night, I was reading the book of Numbers and I realized I don't have yours.

So the only thing left that your eyes haven't said yet is your name.

The Ultimate Book of Cheesy Pick Up Lines

So there you are! I've been looking all over for YOU, the woman of my dreams!

So what haven't you been told tonight?

So, come back to my place, and if you don't like it I swear I'll give you a full refund.

So, I see you eat with utensils. Well, I've got one that I'm just dying to put in your drawers.

So, what do you do for a living besides always making all the men excited and warm all over?

So, you must be the reason men fall in love.

Somebody better call God, because heaven is missing an angel.

Somebody call the cops, because it's got to be illegal to look that good!

The Ultimate Book of Cheesy Pick Up Lines

Somebody needs to call the bomb squad, because you're the bomb.

Someone should call the police, because you just stole my heart!

Someone vacuum my lap, I think this girl needs a clean place to sit.

Sorry, but you owe me a drink. [Why?] Because when I looked at you, I dropped mine.

Sorry, I can't hold on... I've already fallen for you.

Stand still so I can pick you up!

Stop, drop, and roll, baby. You are on fire.

Summer is over because you are just about to fall for me.

Sure, I might be one of the prettiest gal here, but fact is I'm the only one coming over to talk to you.

Tag! You're it! *then pretend to run away*

Tell me if you can handle a real woman.

Tell me, are you are beautiful on the inside as you are on the outside?

That dress looks great on you…as a matter of fact, so would I.

That's a really nice package. Can I help you unwrap it?

That's not a candy cane in my pocket. I'm just glad to see you.

The body is made up of 90% water and I'm thirsty.

The Ultimate Book of Cheesy Pick Up Lines

The more I drink, the prettier you get.

The only thing that you haven't told me yet is your name. So, may I have it?

The Romantic melts in your hands.

The word for tonight is "legs". Let's go back to my place and spread the word.

Then again, I would be too!

There are no seats, can I sit on your face?

There is a big sale in my bedroom tonight. Clothes are 100 % off.

There is something wrong with my cell phone. It doesn't have your number in it.

There isn't a word in the dictionary for how good you look.

There must be a light switch on my forehead because every time I see you, you turn me on!

There must be a rainbow over my head because I've just found my pot of gold.

There must be something wrong with my eyes, I can't take them off you.

There's no doubt we would make sexy babies. I just checked out your profile for the past few days simply trying to come up with a clever message that you encourage you to say, " Just take me know please"…holy crap, I've never worked this hard for a girl ever.

There's only one thing I want to change about you. Your last name.

The Ultimate Book of Cheesy Pick Up Lines

They say a girl's best friend are her legs. But even the best of friends sometimes have to part.

They say dating is a numbers game... so can I get your number?

This isn't a beer belly, It's a fuel tank for a love machine.

This may seem corny, but you make me really horny.

This must be love at first sight because I can't stand the thought of never seeing you again.

This time next year let's be laughing together.

Those are nice jeans, do you think I could get in them.

The Ultimate Book of Cheesy Pick Up Lines

To rate your beauty on a scale from one to nine, I'd rate you as a nine and I'm the one that you need.

Truth be told, you're so much hotter than a sunburn.

Turning off the lights is one of my turn on's.

Turning off you engine, keeps my motor humming.

Vogue just called, they want to put you on the cover.

Wanna ring in the new year with a bang?

Want to get some air? You took my breath away!

Want to get some coffee? 'Cause I like you a latte.

The Ultimate Book of Cheesy Pick Up Lines

Was that an earthquake…. Or did you just rock my world?

Was you father an alien? Because there's nothing else like you on Earth!

Was your Dad a baker? Because you've got a nice set of buns.

Was your dad a boxer? Cause you're a knockout!

Was your dad a farmer? Cause you sure have great melons.

Was your Dad in the Air Force? Because you're da bomb.

Was your dad king for a day? He must have been to make a princess like you.

Was your father a mechanic? Then how did you get such a finely tuned body.

The Ultimate Book of Cheesy Pick Up Lines

Was your father a thief? 'Cause someone stole the stars from the sky and put them in your eyes.

Well, I AM telepathic, and I can tell that you love me. Right? [NO!] Darn, I always get "love" and "lust" mixed up.

Were you arrested earlier? It's gotta be illegal to look that good.

Were you born to be cute or you had to work at it?

Were you in Boy Scouts? Because you sure have tied my heart in a knot.

Were your parents Greek Gods, 'cause it takes two gods to make a goddess.

What are the odds of you being in my favor?

What are you doing for the rest of your life? Because I want to spend it with you.

What are you doing tonight? Besides me, of course?

What do I have to do to get on your drunk dial list?

What do you like for breakfast?

What do you think about us taking a picture? I just want to make sure Santa Claus knows what I want for Christmas this year.

What do you want for Christmas? A date with me!

What does it feel like to be the most beautiful girl in this room?

What is your favorite flower? I'd like to get you one.

What is your gpa?

What pickup line actually works on you?

What size shoe do you wear? Oh, let me guess. It's size sexy, isn't it?

What time do you get off? Can I watch?

What time do you have to be back in heaven?

What'cha doing for the rest of your life?

What's your name? Or can I call you "mine"?

What's a beautiful girl like you doing in a place like this?

What's that on your face? Oh, must just be beauty. Here, let me get it off. Hey, it's not coming off!

What's that perfume you're wearing? Because it's hypnotized me.

The Ultimate Book of Cheesy Pick Up Lines

When God made you, he was showing off.

When I first saw you I looked for a signature, because every masterpiece has one.

When I first saw you, I knew we could win the Stanley Cup in tonsil hockey.

When I look at you, you make me want to wish I wasn't gay.

When I look into your eyes, it is like a gateway into the world of which I want to be a part.

When I see you, the sea levels are not the only ones rising…

When I'm older, I'll look back at all of my crowning memories, and I'll think of the day my children were born, the day I got married, and the day that I met you.

The Ultimate Book of Cheesy Pick Up Lines

Where do you hide your halo?

Where do you hide your wings?

Where have you been hiding because I've been looking for you for ages.

Which is easier? You getting into those tight pants or getting you out of them?

Why don't you surprise your roommate and not come home tonight

With my IQ and your body, we could make a race of superchildren and conquer the earth!

Would you grab my arm so I can tell my friends I've been touched by an angel?

Would you like Gin and platonic, or do you prefer Scotch and sofa?

The Ultimate Book of Cheesy Pick Up Lines

Would you like to help a homeless? If yes, will you take me home?

Wouldn't we look cute on a wedding cake together?

Wow, you must be a real dictator because I'm experiencing an uprising.

Wow...You workout, don't you?

Yesterday, I saw a radiant flower and thought it was the most precious thing I had ever seen, that was until I met you.

You are a 9 - you'd be a perfect 10 if you were with me.

You are cute, I am cute...Let's go to your place and be cute together.

The Ultimate Book of Cheesy Pick Up Lines

You are like my favorite cup of coffee, hot and lip smacking!

You are like my own personal brand of heroin.

You are pretty much perfect. If I could change anything the only thing I would change would be your last name.

You are so beautiful that you give the sun a reason to shine.

You are so fine, I wish I could plant you and grow a whole field of you.

You are so hot that you would make the devil sweat.

You are so hot, it's girls like you that are the real reason for global warming.

The Ultimate Book of Cheesy Pick Up Lines

You are so sweet that you are giving me a toothache.

You are sweet enough to cure me of my addiction to lollies.

You are the reason men fall in love.

You auto-complete me!

You be the Dairy Queen and I'll be your Burger King: You treat me right, and I'll do it your way.

You better call Life Alert, 'cause I've fallen for you and I can't get up.

You better stop drinking now because you're still going to drive me home.

You bring new meaning to the word "edible".

The Ultimate Book of Cheesy Pick Up Lines

You can call me "The Fireman", mainly because I turn the hoes on.

You can call me cake, cause I'll go straight to your butt.

You can kiss me if I'm wrong but I'm pretty sure your name is…Robert?

You can't be my first, but I want you to be my last.

You don't have a ring? Someone should already have snatched you up.

You don't need keys to drive me crazy.

You had better phone the firefighters in advance, cause when you're done with me, we'll be on fire!

You have beautiful eyes. Can I just sit here and stare at them?

You're on Page 141 - have you found your favorite Pick Up Line Yet?

The Ultimate Book of Cheesy Pick Up Lines

You have been very naughty. Go to my room!

You have some nice jewelry. It would look great on my nightstand.

You hear that, the ocean wants you to join me for a drink.

You just made my dopamine all silly.

You know how they say skin is the largest organ on the human body? Not in my case.

You know I'd like to invite you over, but I'm afraid you're so hot that you'll skyrocket my air-conditioning bill.

You know the more I drink, the prettier you get!

You know what they say about men with big feet. Want to prove that to me?

The Ultimate Book of Cheesy Pick Up Lines

You know what would look great on you? Me!

You know what you and the weather have in common? You're both hot.

You know what you would look totally beautiful in? Simply put…my arms.

You know what you'd look great in? My arms.

You know you like me so let's not pretend anymore.

You know you're in love when you can't fall asleep because reality is finally better than your dreams.

You know, Dr. Phil says I'm afraid of commitment...Want to help prove him wrong?

You know, I would die happy if I saw you naked just once!

You're on Page 143 - have you found your favorite Pick Up Line Yet?

You know, you might be asked to leave soon. You're making the other women look really bad.

You look beautiful today, just like every other day.

You look delicious—can I have a lick?

You look exactly like my future ex-wife.

You look familiar, didn't we take a class together? I could've sworn we had chemistry.

You look familiar. Did you graduate from 'The University of Handsome Men'?

You look like a cool glass of refreshing water, and I am the thirstiest man in the world.

You look like a lost angel. Can I take you to heaven?

You look like my third wife. [how many time have you been married?] Twice.

You look like the girlfriend I have in my dreams.

You look like the icing on the cake and I would love to have a taste.

You look like you need a company, I am here to serve you.

You look lonely, would you like company?

You look so familiar… did we take a class together? No? I could've sworn you and I had chemistry.

You look ugly but I still want to get to know you.

You make me melt like hot fudge on a sundae.

The Ultimate Book of Cheesy Pick Up Lines

You make me wish I weren't gay!

You may be asked to leave soon, you're making all the other women look bad.

You may fall from the sky, you may fall from the tree, but the best way to fall....is in love with me.

You might be asked to leave soon. You are making the other women look bad.

You must be a broom, 'cause you just swept me off my feet.

You must be a hell of a thief because you stole my heart from across the room."

You must be a high test score, because I want to take you home and show you to my mother.

You must be a keyboard, because you're just my type.

The Ultimate Book of Cheesy Pick Up Lines

You must be a magician, because every time I look at you, everyone else disappears.

You must be a ninja, because you snuck into my heart.

You must be a very important textbook passage, because seeing you is the highlight of my day.

You must be a vodka shot, because you hit me hard and spun my world around.

You must be from Jamaica. Because "Jamaican" me crazy.

You must be from Pearl Harbor, because baby, you're the bomb.

You must be in the wrong place, the Miss Universe contest is over there

You must be Jelly, cause jam don't shake like that.

The Ultimate Book of Cheesy Pick Up Lines

You must be the one for me. Because my permeable membrane let you through and you know how selective that membrane is.

You must be the reason for global warming—you are so hot!

You must be the wind because you've just swept me off my feet.

You must be tired, because you've been running through my mind all night!

You must do interior design because you definitely made this room more beautiful.

You put the X in sexy! You put the L in love. :)

You really shouldn't wear any make up. Because it would just mess up the perfection.

You're on Page 148 - have you found your favorite Pick Up Line Yet?

The Ultimate Book of Cheesy Pick Up Lines

You remind me of a magnet, because you sure are attracting me over here!

You remind me of an overdue library book, because you've got 'Fine' written all over you.

You Say: "Sorry, I can't hold on... I've already fallen for you."

You seem so content. But you also seem to be quite alone here. So, can I disrupt your reverie?

You should be someone's wife.

You should join the circus.(Why?) So you can learn to juggle the balls all day.

You shouldn't wear makeup. It's messing with perfection!

You spend so much time in my mind, I should charge you rent.

You're on Page 149 - have you found your favorite Pick Up Line Yet?

You wanna know what's the best thing in my life? It's the first word of this sentence

You wanna know what's beautiful? Read the first word again.

You were awesome on television last night.

You: "Did it hurt?" Her: "Did what hurt?" You: "When you fell from Heaven?"

You: "Excuse me, you dropped something" Her: "What?" You: "My jaw."

You: "I'm invisible. Can you see me?" Her: "uh.. yeah?" You: "What about tomorrow night?"

You: "Sorry, but you owe me a drink." Her: "What? Why?" You: "Well, when I saw you, I dropped mine."

You: Your father must have been a thief. Huh? Because he stole the stars from the sky and put them in your eyes.

You'd better direct that beauty somewhere else or you'll set the carpet on fire."

You're a drug. I'm an addict. I'm gonna have to check into rehab tomorrow

You're a real health hazard, you're so sweet you'll be giving me diabetes soon.

You're everything I thought I never wanted.

You're hotter than donuts grease.

You're kinda, sorta, basically, pretty much always on my mind.

You're like my underwear. I can't last a day without you.

The Ultimate Book of Cheesy Pick Up Lines

You're like pizza. Even when you are bad, you're good.

You're like Pringles once I pop you, I can't stop you.

You're like the lyrics to my favorite song; hard to forget and always on my mind.

You're my favorite weakness.

You're not a vegetarian, are you? Because I'd love to meat you.

You're on my list of things to do tonight.

You're single? I'm single. Coincidence? I think not.

You're so attractive that my phone gets hot just from talking to you.

The Ultimate Book of Cheesy Pick Up Lines

You're so beautiful that you made me forget my pickup line."

You're so beautiful, even the leaves fall for you.

You're so cute it's distracting!

You're so hot, even my pants are falling for you!

You're so hot, I could bake cookies on you.

You're so hot, you'd make the devil sweat

You're so sweet, you're giving me a toothache.

You're the cream and l want to be the cherry on top

You're the prettiest girl I've ever seen, and I understand, that you may be too sober to find me attractive… in that case, allow me to buy you a drink

You've got to be tuckered out because you've been running through my mind all night long.

You'd better direct that beauty somewhere else, you'll set the carpet on fire.

You'll do.

Your ass is so nice that it is a shame that you have to sit on it.

Your belt looks extremely tight. Let me loosen it for you.

Your body is 75 % water and I'm thirsty.

Your body is a wonderland, and I'd like to be Alice.

The Ultimate Book of Cheesy Pick Up Lines

Your butt is so nice that it is a shame that you have to sit on it.

Your clothes look uncomfortable. Take them off right now!

Your daddy must have been a hunter because you're a fox!

Your eyes are as blue as the ocean. And baby, I'm lost at sea.

Your face reminds me of a wrench, every time I think of it my nuts tighten up.

Your legs must be tired because you've been running through my mind all night.

Your lips look like wine and I wanna get drunk!

Your lips look lonely. Let me introduce them to mine.

The Ultimate Book of Cheesy Pick Up Lines

Your name must be Pepsi (or Coca-Cola). Because you are so delicious.

Your name must be yogurt, because I wanna spoon you.

Your shirt has to go, but you can stay

Your smile puts the city lights to shame. You're cute.

You're cute—can I keep you?

You're hotter than donut grease.

You're hotter than Papa Bear's porridge.

You're kinda, sorta, basically, pretty much always on my mind.

The Ultimate Book of Cheesy Pick Up Lines

You're like a dictionary, you add meaning to my life!

You're like pizza. Even when you are bad, you're good

You're looking a little cold. Would you like to use me as a blanket?

You're single. I'm single. Coincidence? I think not.

You're so beautiful that you made me forget my pickup line.

You're so hot you would make the devil sweat.

You're so hot you're melting my mind!

You're so hot, I bet you could light a candle at 10 paces.

You're on Page 157 - have you found your favorite Pick Up Line Yet?

The Ultimate Book of Cheesy Pick Up Lines

You're so hot, I could bake cookies on you.

You're the cream and I want to be the cherry on top.

You're the kind of girl I would love to introduce to my parents.

You're the kind of girl I've been waiting all my life to spoil.

You're the one I've been wishing on a star for.

You're the only girl I love now... but in ten years, I'll love another girl. She'll call you 'Mommy.'

You've been naughty! Go to my room.

Printed in Great Britain
by Amazon